Do Animals Talk?

By Mary Lindeen

Scott Foresman
is an imprint of

Glenview, Illinois • Boston, Massachusetts • Chandler, Arizona •
Upper Saddle River, New Jersey

Photographs

Every effort has been made to secure permission and provide appropriate credit for photographic material. The publisher deeply regrets any omission and pledges to correct errors called to its attention in subsequent editions.

Unless otherwise acknowledged, all photographs are the property of Pearson Education, Inc.

Photo locators denoted as follows: Top (T), Center (C), Bottom (B), Left (L), Right (R), Background (Bkgd)

Opener ©Wild Images Ltd./Getty Images; **1** ©Cyril Laubscher/DK Images; **3** ©Kennan Ward/Corbis; **4** (TL) ©Corbis/SuperStock, (BL) ©Wild Images Ltd./Getty Images, (TR) ©UpperCut Images/SuperStock, (BR) Martin Harvey/Gallo Image/Corbis; **5** ©Scott Camazine/Photo Researchers, Inc.; **6** ©Tartan Dragon Ltd/Getty Images, **7** ©W. Perry Conway/Corbis; **8** ©Jose Luis Pelaez, Inc./Corbis; **9** ©Masterfile (Royalty-Free Div.), **10** ©Ron Cohn, koko.org, the Gorilla Foundation/Newscom; **11** ©AP Images; **12** ©Ron Cohn, koko.org, the Gorilla Foundation/Newscom; **13** ©Manuela Hartling/Reuters/Corbis; **14** ©Cyril Laubscher/DK Images; **15** ©2008 Jupiterimages Corporation; **16** ©dimis/Fotolia.

ISBN 13: 978-0-328-47288-8
ISBN 10:   0-328-47288-3

Copyright © by Pearson Education, Inc., or its affiliates. All rights reserved. Printed in the United States of America. This publication is protected by copyright, and permission should be obtained from the publisher prior to any prohibited reproduction, storage in a retrieval system, or transmission in any form or by any means, electronic, mechanical, photocopying, recording, or likewise. For information regarding permissions, write to Pearson Curriculum Rights & Permissions, One Lake Street, Upper Saddle River, New Jersey 07458.

Pearson® is a trademark, in the U.S. and/or in other countries, of Pearson plc or its affiliates.
Scott Foresman® is a trademark, in the U.S. and/or in other countries, of Pearson Education, Inc., or its affiliates.

3 4 5 6 7 8 9 10 V010 13 12 11 10

Jane Goodall is a scientist who studies animals. She worked in Africa where she observed chimpanzees. She learned many things about chimps that no one had known before.

Goodall learned that chimps use simple tools, such as twigs, for getting food. She also learned that they communicate with one another. Chimps use their faces and voices to "talk" to each other.

Many other scientists have studied the ways animals share information about food, shelter, and enemies with one another. For example, bees "dance" to tell one another exactly where food is.

Other researchers study the sounds whales make. Humpback whales and some blue whales make repeated sounds to tell one another where food is or to find a mate. These sounds are called *whale songs*.

Prairie dogs live in large "towns" underground. Scientists have observed that they make alarm calls to warn one another of nearby enemies. They even have different alarm calls for different enemies!

Many scientists have wondered whether animals can communicate with people using language. Of course, we already know the meaning of some animal sounds. When a cat purrs, it usually means that the cat is happy. When a dog growls and bares its teeth, we know it's angry or scared.

Many people believe that animals understand words we speak to them as well. Some even wonder whether it would be possible for animals and humans to learn the same language. That way, we could speak back and forth to one another.

Scientists have done many experiments to try to prove that humans and animals can "talk" to each other. Have you ever heard of a gorilla named Koko?

Koko has learned more than 1,000 words in sign language. Her trainer, Dr. Penny Patterson, began teaching Koko sign language when the gorilla was just a baby.

Some people believe Koko is talking to Dr. Patterson. Others believe Koko has simply been trained to use gestures she doesn't really understand. Everyone agrees, however, that Koko is a very smart gorilla!

Another scientist worked with a dog named Rico. She proved that Rico knew the names of more than 200 toys and could understand simple sentences. However, while Rico seemed to know what people said to him, he could not use words to tell people what he was thinking or feeling.

Parrots can use their voices to make noises that sound like human words. One researcher taught Alex, an African gray parrot, to answer simple questions. Some people say that Alex is just copying sounds he has heard. Others believe Alex understands what he's saying and is really talking.

Dolphins can't talk because they don't have vocal cords. They communicate with clicks, squeaks, and whistles. Some scientists have tried making these same sounds to communicate with dolphins, but so far, only dolphins can talk with dolphins.

We know for sure that animals communicate with one another. But will animals and humans be able to truly "talk" together someday too? Will there be a new language? What do you think animals will want to tell us?